Still Water Words

Poems and Stories from Ancestral Places

Patricia Ann West

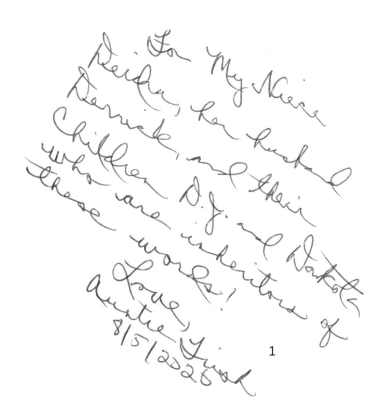

For My Niece
Keisha, her husband
Derrick, and their
Children D.J. and Dakota
who are inheritors of
these words!
Love,
Auntie Trish
8/5/2020

1

ISBN: 9781694536198 Paperback

ASIN: B0862HL5KY Kindle

Independently Published

For inquiries:

Contact authorpatwest@gmail.com

Facebook: Author Patricia Ann West

Printed in the United States of America

Contents

Dedication

Still Water Words: Poems and Stories from Ancestral Places is dedicated to those strong and heroic ancestors who survived the journeys across transatlantic waters, through turbulent years, and to those relations left behind on African shores who helped them pack the cultural treasures that have survived. Thanks to my parents, Anna Bell Smalls and Elijah West, Sr. and their families in Parker's Ferry, Charleston, SC, and Bellinger Hill, SC for the DNA in these deep, still water words.

Acknowledgements

The first group deserving my deep gratitude is that of the dynamic storytellers in my families from the Ferry to the Hill in the state of South Carolina. These are members of the Smalls out of Charleston and Parker's Ferry and the Scott-West family out of Beaufort and Jasper counties. There are a few in particular that are responsible for what I have written, namely Anna Bell Smalls West, Rosalee Smalls Simmons, Robert Smalls, Sr., Robert Smalls, Jr. ,Nathaniel Smalls, Doris Johnson Frazier, Norris Smalls, Mabel Scott Anderson, and my cousin-like-brother, Freddie L. West. Although my parents, cousins Cornelius 'Baby' Scott, Richard West, Norris Smalls, Aunt Rosalee, and Uncle Benjamin Franklin West, Sr. have passed on, they left imprints in this collection and enough material for more verses and prose to follow. I thank each of these named relatives for teaching me about the past with their ways of talking, joking, laughing, teaching, and fighting back tears. Or, just fighting back!

Thanks to my family, friends, and fellow writers who gave the project uplift. Such encouragement came from cousins Leroy West, Susan Rivers, and Reggie Singleton, among the first who laid eyes on early drafts and let me know that they ordained sharing the stories in the way they are told. Susan had a sharp eye for the smallest of errors and I appreciate that. My friend Ellen Hallstrom Ryan added keen insights on the book description. My neighbor Rachel Smith and my siblings were there during a medical challenge along the way and in recent times to help me when needed. Much appreciation to Diane West, Nathaniel Coxon, Cynthia West Baker, Earl Coxon, Elijah West, Jr., Elaine West, Kenneth West, Sr., Kathy West Lee, Travis West, and sister/niece Kimberly West. Even though our sister Pamela West has passed on, she played her part in story-making while good and alive! I can see and hear her genuine, good-hearted laughter in reaction to some of the pieces!

Friend and writing colleague Darrell Gartrell encouraged this project from the beginning and kept sending me messages to essentially 'report' my progress. Each inquiry acted as a nudge for me to get to work.

The most valuable feedback came from friend and my Gullah Geechee spiritual kin person, Alex Barr. As a child of the Gullah region, Alex not only knows and understands the culture, but is blessed with a wonderful writing voice of his own. Thank you so much!

Early on I decided to use vintage family photographs and two public domain documents to add information and context to my words. I would like to thank each person who gave their blessing to publish pictures from their family records. Special thanks to cousins Theresa Scott Vanardo, Susan Rivers, Louise Drayton Hamilton, and church sister Wilmotine Brisbane Ellis. All other photos are from my parents' collection or taken by me.

And finally, I acknowledge my husband Stephen Gairn from his native Australia, his Southern hemisphere, but who appreciates *my* history, *my* food, *my* people, *our* struggles! To my son Dedan Kinyatti McClinton and grandson, Dedan Kimathi McClinton, Ma Dukes /Grandma Pat thanks you both for your love and devotion!

Introduction

"Still waters run deep." That's what my father would say as family members and neighbors would make remarks about me, such as "She sho is quiet." "Trish don' neva say nothin." I did not understand it at the time, but now I realize that my brain was forever turning; I was listening to adults talk about the funny, the sad, or things yet to be. Being quiet made me feel like a misfit—different, yet protected in my world. Elijah West, Sr. spoke those words in defense of his daughter whose difference he recognized. My mother, Anna Bell Smalls West, likewise, realized that I preferred paper, pencils, and coloring books with the alphabet rather than getting my hands and clothes dirty playing outside in the yard.

About 7th grade, I discovered the library at Johnson Junior High and a book about the Little Rock Nine. My teacher sent me there for some time out, I believe, because she had tried everything else to spark my learning. Before that, I just concentrated on making the grades from the old hand-me-down, raggedy textbooks from the all-white schools. Did she sense boredom? After all, I was a reader since first grade. My teacher Hubert Elementary, Mrs. Richardson, would send me to the other teachers to read to their classes. I loved to act out the words and make them come alive with expression! So by 7th

grade, that one more advanced book about my own people led to another and another--like food I had to consume to live! Mrs. Helen Riley, the school librarian at Johnson, pulled books on African kings and queens, history, and just good reading in general. I began to go even deeper in my thoughts and I began to write down phrases and ideas that would just pop into my head. Donald Murray [1] would say that I was "rehearsing" my writing. In a two-bedded square room shared with my sisters Diane, Cynthia, and Pam, I carved out a spot to sit and write in secret at the foot of the bed about race, slavery, injustice, lynchings, or famous people. My poems became creative reading responses that I would hide away. Sadly, my librarian, Mrs. Riley passed away in 2012 without a 'thank you' from me—until now.

Many of the poems and the creative non-fiction pieces you will read are inspired by what I heard, ate, spoke, and saw in Parker's Ferry, SC. What would I be without recalling Aunt Rosalee

---

[1] Murray, Donald M. "Writing as a Process: How Writing Finds Its Own Meaning." *Eight Approaches to Teaching Composition.* Eds. Timothy R. Donovan and Ben W. McClelland. Urbana: National Council of Teachers of English (NCTE), 1980.

Simmons talk about Uncle Charlie's "stink" foot? What kind of Gullah Geechee descendant would I be without documenting how my Uncle Robert Smalls would "knock de boney" in church?

Others pieces come from growing up near the Savannah River and all the history tied to its ebb and flow.

Closer to the Georgia state line is Bellinger Hill, or B'lingy Hill as my paternal ancestors would say. It carries its own lessons and secrets reflected in this collection. Cummingsville Cemetery, the Scott-West burial ground bought and set aside after Reconstruction, was the place where many stories were told standing around after a funeral. The same can be said of the burial spaces of my maternal ancestors outside Charleston.

What I write is as important as formation and style. What is the best way to honor ancestors who experienced cultural loss? Restore the loss. Therefore, I experiment with forms such as the African praise poem and the African-American poetry form called the eintou, both meant to embrace and privilege Afro-centric forms of writing. I consider the last piece a benediction. "Day Clean" is written in an experimental pattern that I devised based on a West African word for *outcry*, recorded by Gullah linguist and historian

Lorenzo Dow Turner. [2] As I imagine and propose, the *ntata* is a way to raise one's voice in a poetic way against wrongs to make right. In keeping with the elements of orality, it should make use of rhythm, rhyme, and expressions and phrases learned and carried over from the Gullah Geechee culture.

Any place in the African Diaspora can, and does, ignite a poetic response. Whether in Georgia or South Carolina in the Gullah Geechee Heritage Corridor, or visiting Central American and the Caribbean, I was exposed to Africanisms that have survived through centuries. In six sets, I present *My Gullah Geechee Riversides and Roads, People Praisin' Poems and Portraits, Ol' Timey Places and Faces, Reflections from the Diaspora, Still Water Realities: Creative Non-Fiction, and New Days-Day Clean.*

Nothing can bring back those days of walking to the crossroads, picking that sticky okra from Uncle Mose Smalls' yard, skipping rocks down at Penny Creek, hearing Cornelius Scott tell about the day of Jubilee, and eating fresh from B'lingy Hill fields. But, we have new days to pass old ways on to present and future generations. Through these still water words, I take you there.

---

[2] Turner, Lorenzo Dow. *Africanisms in the Gullah Dialect.* 1949. Print.

Gullah Geechee Riversides and Roads

Where I Am From

I am from Henry and Elizabeth Smalls
because they survived the sins of slavery
and saw the sun while free.

I am from Thomas and Daphane Seabrooks
of Seabrooks Plantation,
parents of Diana, grandmother through maternal
blood

born on Edisto Island with Native American blood
mixed with the richness of Africa.
I am from mixed genes with undeniable smooth
dark skin.
I am from men with long, strong legs
and women-- just strong!

I am from
Peter, Moses, Sam, Jr., Elizabeth, Henry, Isaac,
Robert, Rosalee, Eugene, Joseph, Rebecca,
Harrison, and Anna.

I am from Big Al' in the spirit
who lived up Sugar Hill and
I am from Uncle Charlie and stories about his stink
foot.

I am from preachin' and prayin' on Sundays,
farming and fishing,
hunting and smokin' meats.
I am from growing and picking' peas, beans, and
greens.
I am from sloppin' hogs, milking cows, and
feeding roosters and chickens to feed me.
I am from priming rusty red pumps,
Walking to the outhouse in the light,
Using the chamber pot at night--
rinsing it after sunrise.

I am from 'shine and homemade elderberry wine,
Crying, lying, and testifyin'.
I am from every speck of dirt from
the Crossroads to Penny Creek,
I am from the railroad tracks,
o'ver bridge,
the woods,
and the river.

I am from
Knock 'de boney,
Amen!
"I'll fly away",
"The Lord's Prayer" chanted
and the New Year Shout.
I am from staying up all night with coffins
And women wailing for our dead.

This is our family, our land, our past---
Where I,
we are from.

To Be Sold

A Docu-Poem

The fifth day of May, 1761
To be sold at Parker's Ferry
Twenty and more of my   kind
Great, Great blood line
Gone forever!
Names changed, children lost
Because they were "valuable SLAVES"
In St. Paul's Parish.
Women, carpenters, and boatmen in bondage
Announced for sale to slave traders in *The Carolina Gazette.*
Dates marked; slave holders setting clocks
To trade valuable humans suffering with small pox!

10 to be sold!
40 to be sold!
Like a party invitation, its ink was pressed for
auction news.
Acres for good rice land, corn, and indigo on settled
plantations.
Invited to inspect and buy twenty and more of my
kin, Yet no reparations come from buyer blood lines
whose surnames we
 sign today, forced to hide our own heritage.
We suffer from imagined visions of those auction
days

  —when we read street signs
  —when we cross town borders, one after the
other
  Named for those who sold sisters and
brothers.
  To be sold, all sold
  To be lost, all lost.

*A Slave Auction at Parker's Ferry, SC. Clipping is
from The South Carolina Gazette, Charles-Town,
April 25, 1761, front page*

De Ol' people Say: *Nana's Knock 'de Boney Lesson*

A Performable Text with Stick, Hands, or Tambourine

This is the sound that will call you back home.
> This is the drum beat you should not forget.
> " De ol' people say they brought this all de
> way from Africa."
> They say, "Never forget, never forget."
> "Pass it on, Pass it on."

O'er bridge, in the church, on Penny Creek Road,
> In fly away music on Sunday morn.
> They say, "Never forget; never forget."
> "Pass it on. Pass it on."
> This is the shout for New Year's Eve night.
> Go in a circle, a circle that's tight.
> Step children step; do not ever forget.
> "Pass it on; pass it on."
> *Clap it out! Clap it out!*
> *Clap! Clap! Clap! Clap! Clap!*
> *Clap! Clap! Clap! Clap! Clap!*

Knock de boney, knock de bone, knock 'de bone!
Knock de boney, knock de bone, knock 'de bone!
> *Rap! Rap! Rap! Rap! Rap !*
> *Rap! Rap! Rap! Rap! Rap !*

Passed on by Anna Bell Smalls West, 'Nana'

18

Penny Creek

Penny Creek flows free at Parker's Ferry,
just as it did long ago when Native
Cousins stood on its banks
Off the Edisto—
Long black river
Nature's Jewel,
A diversion from Charleston city life, our
Ace Basin beauty.

No fish in sight today.
Images abound,
Sounds surround,
Whether a
Misty morning or ghostly moon.
All's well with
Lily pads for birds to light
And for ancient spirits to linger in
South Carolina sunshine or
Dead at night.

This photo of Penny Creek by Patricia A. West inspires the title.

People Praisin' Poems and Portraits

Miss Janie's Beauty Secrets

It was in Miss Janie's household
Parlor of Beauty
That little girls watched women change.
Black-haired, brown-haired, gray-haired,
blue-rinsed women
We heard converse around the living room
sink.
I'd like to say we overheard
Politics, religion, and history
In attribution to how we now think.
But, it was rather, "Kicked her butt!"
"Who said what?"
When? Where? Why?
Who died? Who lied? or
"Y'all go back outside."

Stories in secret code were spoken.
Words into letters b-r-o-k-e-n.

Through the years,
We learned the words,
Lived their stories retold,
Changed our hair, and
Saw the mysteries unfold.

Miss Mattie's Pork and Beans and Grits

When she fed us

We didn't know

The pork and beans and grits

Meant poverty to social analysts.

To four children,

It was a delicious stomach full!

Mama's Spirit

It is Mama's
spirit
That stirs me up,
Puts the fire in
my heart,
Attitude in my
tongue,
 passion in my
pen.

It is Mama's
spirit
That reminds me how to survive—
How to pay a piece here and a piece there
To make ends meet.
It is her spirit that continues to sing in faith, for
"How Great Thou Art!

It is Mama's spirit
That speaks to me about holding on to
Her precious homeplace—Parker's Ferry.
Laugh! Dance! Enjoy life! Cook enough food!
Don't wait 'til the last minute!
Hold on to your pocketbook!
Get together for the holidays!

It is Mama' spirit
That continues to echo
Her last words that would carry me,
Lift me up, and strengthen me:
"Everything is going to be alright."

My mother, Anna Bell Smalls West, 1926-2003

Elijah's Silent Stories

        In silence, the picture hangs of a young
farmer,
        Grandson of slave ancestors,
        Ready to embark for a voyage to Europe by
sea
        To preserve what America calls 'Liberty.'

        In silence, the picture hangs
        Of a black man in a bronzed helmet
        That perhaps saved his life

Destined to return.
He holds his M1 gun, now rusted and
disarmed,
Fired in defense of freedoms—
Some granted, then denied.

In silence, the picture hangs
To remind us of his front-porch "only
grown-ups" stories:
In England, they would call out and laugh,
"Where's your tail, black boy?

In Germany, battles were fought and
honored
With General Patton's letter mailed home.
"Put this in a frame and keep it for me," he
wrote to his mother Lucile.

In silence the picture hangs
Years after the taps,
The ceremony of a gun salute
and a perfectly folded flag.

Now the marble stands in silence
At the head of his grave
which simply reads,
"Corporal West
U.S. Army
World War II."

For my father, Elijah West, Sr., 1923-1991

Sincerely, Maggie

From Bellinger Hill I made many journeys.
From Nin's womb in 1919, by rivers, by
roads,
I would leap into the decade of
New Negroes fleeing
The sight of rope stretched necks
and bodies bleeding.

Nin and Father Richard would be my first
teachers
at Mt. Zion Presbyterian Church.
From there, I was prepared for new
knowledge to search.
With sisters Emma and Ernestine, I would
journey
to answer roll call at Penn School built for
Reconstruction,
once served by Charlotte Forten.
To St. Helena, we went by boat across the
river.
In heat we would sweat; in cold we would
shiver.

We had to learn numbers, readin', writin',
        science, cookin', sewin', and nursin'
Or, whatever we were taught.

After all, just one generation before, Ma
Grace and Father Bob
Had been bought and freedom-robbed.

So, with my lessons behind,
I took another journey as part of the
"Great Migration" from South to North.
Oh, we traveled unafraid because someone
said New York had jobs
And Old Jim Crow was dead.
I took myself there like a woman blind
While I was young, pretty, and refined.
Just look at how I was blessed.
Looked like a million dollars in my high
class dress!

Mama, Daddy, and brothers were left in
Carolina
Just a telegram wire away.
I became a wife, mother, and grandmother.
But I never forgot how to spot mistletoe
high up a grand oak, nor
Nin's love for yellow daffodils
Planted in the homestead yard
To bloom after winter's chill.

Now family, I am on my last journey
Loved all I can love,
Been all I could ever be.

For Aunt Maggie West Robinson

One Day

An Oral History Poem

He was born
one day in
1931,

during the
historic Great
Migration.
As a son in B'lingy Hill, Richard was raised
with the Gullah folkways.
He was more than a grandson to Bubba and Lucile.
        Instead of cities in New York, with busses,
traffic, and trains,
        he learned about the farms, fields, and
rivers.
        He loved his uncles Benjamin (Ruby), Lige,
Harold, Moses, and Nathaniel as brothers
        And in later life adopted 'Ruby' as a father
figure.
        He was a walking witness to African
American history
        Proud as the grandson of a black man who
could read in B'lingy Hill,

        For Great-grandma Jane, as she lay ill--

He said, "I took her coffee first thing in the morning."
When she knock with the stick,
I go pump the pump 'til de water get cool."

He was there to hear Ma Jane groan,
"Mmmmmm, mmmm"
He was there to receive her last words, "I'm gonna leave;
I'm gonna leave y'all now."
He was there to hear Lucile, wail, "Oh, ma!"
"Oh, ma!"
He was there as Jane, a former slave, drifted off to freedom, eyes cast on the Bright and Morning Star.

Richard West loved to tell stories and you knew you'd get a good one when he started with the words,
"One day…"
His mind was sharp as a needle from a swingin' pine as he worked words into patterns, and sounds,
As someone knitting a shrimp net.

In and out he would go. Would not forego who did what, where, why, and when.
He'd laugh at himself and laugh with you at the story's end.
One day, he said, "I gone into the barn to get corn to feed de mule;
I thought a 'skeeter bit me.

Then I see that snake raise 'e head where
Ruby had that car tire— ready to strike again."
I holler and that snake gon' to the pump,
must be to wash 'e mout out.
And I run to the house to my granddaddy."
He told how granddaddy Bubba tied a live
frog around that foot and buried it in the ground 'til
Ruby come home to take him to the doctor.
Before the day of the snake bite, Richard
laughed and said he used to catch live snakes.
"Tie a string on it and just lead 'em around.
Just for fun."
After the bite, he said, the snake adventures
were done.

Richard was an expert in many notions:
Learned how to knit fish nets from No. 9
nylon yarn.
Old man King Washington
Knew how to make the needle from a
hickory stick,
And said, so could all of Julia German[3]
churn, the girls and the boys.
But he boasted that on netting, he was most
fit—
"I can shut my eye and knit."

Richard knew secrets of the woods,
He could talk about safe passage on the path
to light church—

---

[3] One of the 13 children of Ma Jane's son, Robert Scott, Jr.
Several of Julia German's children are still living today with
memory of this skill!

no, not night church—"Light Church"
If church was held after dark, they would
swing a tightened, lighted lantern
To scare the snakes away.
Can't you see him swinging that light high
to get the ol' folks by?
Talking trash to the snakes in the woods?

Richard was blessed with God's grace
during his 82-year race.
He would testify that one day when nearly
all died--he survived.
He could tell you that he was lost-- then
found,
When for months he went missing among
migrant workers.

For almost a year, he reigned as the
patriarch of the West family tree—
A title he held proudly and respectably.
So thank you Richard, for the stories,
For the new pages of black history you will
help us to write,
Thank you for the good times as the oldest
first cousin.
We are promised a great family reunion
meeting; we will see you again—

one day.

*Note: No one knows how Ruby became the nickname for
someone named Benjamin, but that is how my father and
his siblings referred to their older brother.*

Cousin Gallie

Henrietta
Williams was her
certificate name,
Daughter of
Grand Aunt Sue
West—
sister of my
grandfather

Richard, Bubba.

To us she was always Cousin Gallie!

Didn't know Death made her a left alone mother;

didn't know her hurts and harms.

She was a like a warrior woman;

Better not lay no blame!

She was tough and strong--

Scaring us churn talkin' 'bout

"The devil out there in that backyard."

But she had ways to show her sweet side—

Making us pans of molasses-laden sweet potato

pone

and jars of that homemade sweet red wine,

fermented from Bellinger Hill plums,

Always ready by Christmas.

Cousin Gallie kept that head covered, African-style

whenever we went to visit a while,

standing in that small front room--

what-not and knick-knack filled.

To the City of Savannah,

She was a 'colored laundress"

at 631 President Street, East—

no wine, no charms or harms, no devils in the back

yard.

Photo provided by Susan Rivers: Henrietta

"Gallie" Williams holding her daughter Mamie

Ancestry.com. *U.S. City Directories, 1822-1995* [database on-line]. Provo, UT, USA: Ancestry.com Operations, Inc., 2011.

Barefoot Maggie

To our young minds, it was
a thrill, a treat
to see" Barefoot Maggie"
Standing on the corner of Oglethorpe and
Price Streets
to oblige our wandering eyes
during Day-dee's afternoon drive.
In the Ol'Fort and nearby she traveled.
Shoes were never the matter.
In rain, in cold, in rising Savannah heat,
Shoes were always refused.
Now, I wonder about Maggie
And her amazing feat.
She must have looked back down the river
That brought our ancestors
And held on to some innate memory from
faraway
Where tall, bronzed women like Maggie
Walk in bare feet
Upon warm
Black
Soil.

Miss Scrappy
Caroline Butler Wright

That Miss Scrappy!
Short, black, and sassy,
Smiled sweetly,
Laughed deeply,
Stepped lively all over Savannah's streets
From Boundary to Arnold to Grove.

Her momma Charity was born in 1865 on the cusp
of slavery's
legal end.
She would cook as a way to fend;
Caroline's work was washerwoman at all those
places marking life,
Working even as Thomas's wife.

That Miss Scrappy could handle hot water washing
for whites
and for darks, water clean and cool.
It was the best she could do with only four years of
school
as Charity's baby born in 1889 during
Reconstruction.

Before they laid Miss Scrappy down in Laurel
Grove's colored section in 1975,
She, Caroline B. Wright, had become like a
surrogate grandmother
walking bags of hand-me-downs to neighborhood
girls and boys.

The reason to me is now clear that
leftover, not picked up, not paid for
pants, shirts, skirts, and jackets could be worn to
segregated schools
So that my generation could learn lessons way
beyond grade four.

1920; Census Place: Savannah, Chatham, Georgia; Roll: T625_241; Page: 3A; Enumeration District: 83

My brother Kenneth West, Sr. asked the question: Who remembers Miss Scrappy? This is the answer that led to even more questions. Biographical facts are from Ancestry.com

Stirring Culture in Those Cooking Pots:

Savannah's Alongshore Dinner Women

By the time Ol' Hannah the sun rose over the River Savannah

The dinner women were already stirring culture in those cooking pots, loading

food-filled pots, pans, and dishes they remembered from the old people in Parker's Ferry

to satisfy the wishes of hungry longshoremen.

They were men of might and muscle-

Lifting and carrying cargo along the docks,

Unloading goods to go onshore,

Building the shipping industry, boosting a coastal economy,

yet starving for respect.

Despite their good and necessary back-breaking
sacrificial work,

They suffered, restricted from sitting in downtown

luncheonettes and soda grills with all those signs

printed in black and white.

So those dinner women employed themselves,

Cooked for cash or credit collected by

Uncle Joe Johnson and the pistol on his hip.

The dinner women worked along the shores,

delivered baskets of collard greens and hot rice,

something hot or cold to sip,

some beans, some meat for a mid-day meal.

Dinner women like Arene and Carline, and helper
Anna,

though scared of the currents because they could not
swim,

would ride across the water by boat

to set up sidewalk tables dressed in cloths and
flowers—

al fresco dining for sweating black men covered in
cargo dust

waiting for justice to come in decent wages, civil
rights,

good bread and benefits.

*Photo is of my aunt Elizabeth Smalls Johnson, "Auntie
Arine/Irene." Details for this poem come from an oral history
talk with my late Cousin Chief Master Sergeant (Ret.)Norris
Smalls, a Charleston, SC native who retired from the US Air
Force in 1983 and resided in Sacramento, CA until April
2020.Other memories come from Cousin Doris Frazier in
Savannah, GA.*

Uncle Harrison, First Class Prankster

They say, "Harrison Smalls was something else."
Laughed at others; laughed at himself.
It was his nature to enjoy his life.
Helped on the farm as a "plough" hand
Worked at the cotton gin to help his father Sam.

Harrison left Parker's Ferry in 1943,
Had enough of the pickin' and enough of the
plowin.'
He raised his 17-year-old right hand
on April twenty-eighth to swear, "No fear!"
Traded cotton-ginnin' for drilling at Fort Jackson
And answered to Private, World War Two.

He played pranks before earning his rank.
There was the prayer-meeting trick for those taking
the evening walk—going to the church to hear his
father Rev. Smalls talk.
Sneaking from the house on Penny Creek Road,
he'd
pull invisible string across a grassy path and wait
for
victims to trip and call out, "Lord, I fall."

Before he answered to the nickname Shine,
He'd figured out a way to make old folks holler.
Harrison would remove sweet potatoes left to roast
in the fire before they would get too hot for his plot.
Take potato and cut in half; sprinkle red pepper in
the middle.
Put back together, return to fire, laugh and listen for
"Water, Water!"

That was Harrison, and sometimes Thomas,
his closest cousin and accomplice.
They both left us in 1963, but left these stories
To keep us happy and laughing while life lasts.
The next time you take a walk, inspect for string on
the trail
and listen for Harrison whispering, "Check your
sweet potato!"

*Favorite stories often told by Harrison's siblings Robert Smalls, Sr.,
Rosalee Simmons, and Annabell Smalls West. PFC Harrison Smalls
was honorably discharged in 1946 with Victory and Good Conduct
Medals. He served with the famed 240 Port Battalion Company,
Transportation Corps. See Longshore Soldiers: Defying Bombs &
Supplying Victory in a World War II Port by Andrew Brozyna.*

Ol' Timey Places and Faces

13 Dundee

We used to see
Miz Janie pressing hair,
tin roof timbered dwellings
with neighbors taking care,
Green thumbs bragging about their
Devil's backbone,
Mother-in-law tongue,
Wandering Jew,
Miz Bertha stretchin' curtains,
Miz Mattie watching over the churn,
Garbage men getting' their 'Christmas', hot
durn--
Dancin' down Dundee Lane!
Miz Theodosia recitin' Dunbar on Waters at
St. Paul
"When Malindy Sings"--
"The whole thing!"

We used to click-clack,
shoot marbles, losing then coming back.
Crowd Miz Ruth's busy neighborhood store
for shopping,
Hear Annette Dairy's horse-drawn wagon
clopping
On that dusty street
and see white-suited driver
Leaving glass-bottled chocolate milk at your
door,
See the ice man lifting blocks for the ice box
between two huge iron hooks;

46

children peeping or running behind them.
The ve-gee-tuble man calling out "greens,
beans
'maters,' watermelon!"
The rag man collecting what? No-tellin.'

Visions of the time slowly fade out
For the sake of urban renewal phased in--
Neither side knowing what the missing
would mean.

The old Dundee Street home site is now the location of The Tiny House Project serving formerly homeless veterans and has been renamed The Cove at Dundee according to the Chatham-Savannah Authority for the Homeless. This note applies to all the pieces which reflect on Dundee.

Hearse

Did it not seem sane to some soul

In this South that a child pushing for birth

Should have a respectable ride to medical care to
begin life on this earth?

Certainly it seemed crazy

That a powerless and colorless child

Should fall victim to Jim Crow's cruel curse—*[4]

To begin this journey

As it should end—

In a dark, colored hearse.

In 1955, African-Americans in Savannah were transported to a
hospital for blacks by hearse from a black funeral home due to
segregation practices. Such was the entry for my sister, Diane.

Jubilee!

The Scott family slaves were
threshing rice--probably singing a
work song about Jesus Christ, or a
spiritual about laying down
burdens
while separating grains of rice
from the chaff for the sum of
master plus mistress
to profit more as slaves lived on much less.
They were using their skills carried over from our
West African nations
Cameroon and Congo, from Benin, from
Togo and used on Bellinger Hill
plantations.

Born in 1830, Silvy and James
began that day with orders from
from Overseer Lynah to obey.
They had cotton to pick and
baskets to load when they heard
the drums of the union soldiers
As they marched down Bellinger
Hill Road.
My people dropped those tools, stopped those
horses.

Cousin Baby said, "They came running
from the fields." Those in the cabins beat

pots and pans all over that land. They ran
out in the middle of the road.
There was dancing and there was shoutin:
Jubilee! Jubilee!
Liberty! Liberty!
That was the day that
freedom came.
That was the day that
dreams came true—
For you and I to cry
Jubilee! Jubilee! Liberty! Liberty!

This story was related by my cousin, the late Cornelius "Baby" Scott, a grandchild of Jane Cummings Scott and Robert Scott, Sr. who were eyewitnesses to the Jubilee. I learned it from Baby decades ago while visiting Cummingsville Cemetery.

Grace

A Graceful mother-woman sits
Large and regal upon a chair,
A throne of carved mahogany,
brown-colored like the hand that fits
Around the purse clutched above her knee.

A Graceful mother-woman sits
Reflecting on her Father James, Mother Silvy
        Childhood memories of labor forced and
free, just property
Until eighteen-sixty five and the Jubilee.

A Graceful mother-woman sits a century ago
Posed in a studio
Perhaps on the dawn of the 20th century
Like a Gullah queen—serious, serene
Jubilant in new freedoms found
That permitted her to dress up
In hat and shawl ready for church.
Perhaps thinking of a prayer to say
For unseen generations that might see her picture
someday.

        A Graceful mother-woman sits
        In all her Gullah wit
        Reminding us to never quit
        Never forget!

*For my paternal great grand-mother, Jane
Cummings Scott, 1857-1943*

100-Year Walk:

A Praise Poem for Cu'in Maybell

Maybell Simmons Drayton, 1904-2005

Salute to a mother's ancestor!

Carrying the name Simmons since 19 "odd" 4*

Walk grand, Cousin!

At one-hundred years you sat and rocked a while,

History deeply layered behind the smile as you looked on

Parting the holy book.

Cu'in Maybelle, what could you tell? What did you see?

What stories did you take, never shared with family?

Wish I had asked the questions in time,

But didn't know as a child what you could tell.

Just know that Mama always said,

"Make sure y'all go see Cu'in Maybell"

Salute to Cu'in Maybell,

Name proclaimed by 20 "odd' 4 South Carolina lawmakers

Whose predecessors were racist rights takers!

But, you walked through it all, sun up to sun down,

Surviving between Parker's Ferry and Charles-Town

You, living past your centennial year,

Saw your good name inscribed on a state resolution, framed,

And proudly on display for your family to claim!

Photo provided by Cousin Maybell's daughter Louise Drayton Hamilton, "Cousin Loly" of Parker's Ferry, SC

*All my childhood, I heard "odd" stated in the place of zero. This is a colloquial expression for 1904.

A Sonnet for Simon

Simon left Bellinger at the right time.
Born fatefully free after slavery
in eighteen eighty-four facing a climb.
Yet Presbyterians saw bravery.
Not meant for the Great War or cotton fields,
His voice was raised for a black social gospel
from Carolina* pulpits; lives to shield.
He led the young to school, God's apostle.
He cared for kin; made Savannah visits
Even after named Doctor of Divinity.
He was trusted with church business.
First college grad in our Scott family!
Simon left B'lingy; he did not forget.
Work, faith, service shaped life lessons left!

*Grand Uncle Rev.
Simon Herbert
Scott, Sr., D.D.
Feb 24, 1884-January 30, 1965
He is pictured here with his wife, Lena. Photo provided
by daughter Teresa Scott Vanardo and family.*

*Orangeburg, James Island, Johns Island, and Charleston

Walk on Waters

"Walk together
children;

Don't you get weary."[5]

For we have made it to
1898,

33 years from the days
of Jubilee to build a little white house lumbered on
a wet lot—bought cheap.

Previously taken under treaty by Oglethorpe from
its Native Creek,

Bloodied in a battle with the British.

Fields filled with water and priced for Africans to
cultivate rice.

Walk together down Waters Road to Culver; there
you will find

"ST. PAUL'S CHURCH, NEGRO", the records
read.

Eight post-reconstruction soul-folk gathering the
evening before a hurricane

To sustain a life of independence preordained.

---

[5] Words from a Negro Spiritual; author unknown.

To sing, to shout "Hallelujah!" unshackled by an amended Constitution,

To organize institutions, to take care of the colored orphans and the sick,

They were Black Victorians, mastering their fate

In well-suited frock coats and tops hats

To teach, to preach, to raise a roof, to repair steps.

They walked not wearied on Waters,

Working miracles that have lasted through centuries.

Organized in 1898, St. Paul Missionary Baptist Church remains the only building from the late 19th century at the corner of Waters Avenue and Wheaton near downtown Savannah. This 1949 image of St Paul is from the collection of the late Everleatha Brisbane, provided by daughter, Wilmotine B. Ellis.

Contemplation on Bay Street

Under shady, shielding trees

I sit, watch, and contemplate…

Breathing dump truck and tour bus exhaust-fumed

air

filtered by live old oaks and moss,

Listening to soothing cascading water flow,

Piped

through the

mouth of a

stone lion

that graces

the front of

the Old Cotton Exchange

where farmers like grandfather Bubba from B'lingy

Hill

Came to sell their yield.

I watch these tourist wonderers seeking my stories

And indulging in nature near a river that brought

wonderers centuries ago because they, too,

contemplated changes.

I already know the answers to their questions and

The questions which have no answers...

If? Why? Then? Now? When?

I contemplate the possibilities while just sitting

Under a shady, shielding oak

Near the river that flows close to home and

Where my smart 1872 born grandfather— farmer,

Sunday School teacher, and tax collector came to

consign his cotton yield in 1939 when, by fate, *his*

generation was not for sale!

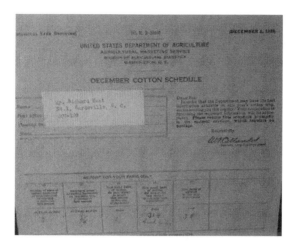

Documents are from the papers of grandfather Richard "Bubba" West, an early family entrepreneur.

Reverberations to a Fireplace, 1960

Mister Andre' Derain artfully drew
 Lines for *Three Nudes in Front of a Fireplace*
To undertake bold color on white space.
 I reflect in this museum milieu
And recall three nudes—of African hue.
A dining room bath, with shy, shamed faces--
Small round washtub; Octagon soap in place,
an old cold Victorian, dollars few.
But Mama warmed water from icy pipes;
carried heavy pots through wintry seasons,
kitchen to tub in front of fire-placed lights.
Now we cruise warm waters for new reasons--
 To erase lines of colored poverty,
 Seek lost identity on islands free.

*French artist Andre' Derain, 1810-1954

Comestibles

The chilly childhood days have passed

When Mama'd light the kitchen stove for heat,

make leftovers for eight-- "somein' to eat"

that would stick to our stomachs and last

'til the next slow water pot wafted past.

Onions, potatoes, neckbones, rice, maybe pig feet

Cornbread, sweet bread, beans, most times no meat.

Prayers on her knees--"How Great Thou Art! Holdfast!

Now hungry days return like a haunting ghost

despite centralized heat, technology, titles,

possessions, and a peek of the world.

Knocked down, I stir— strengthened by genealogical hosts.

After breathing life with less,

I get up again and survive because tough mothers matter!

For Allen

I played half-rubber
and shot pretty colored marbles
in the Dundee Street dust
because he taught me how.

He held my hand
To cross the street and
Let a little girl
Walk to church beside the high school drum major.

Was it the years and the distance, or a
Terrible mistake in judgment?
Was it just plain neglect, or ignorance
and fear that kept me away
From his bedside,
From holding *his* hand,
From walking alongside *him*?

The answers are late and no longer matter.
I
Let
Him
Go
Alone.

Sisters on a Sunday Morning

Before life got real through the years,

Before major life lessons,

Before rats in the house,

Before our dog Skippy died,

Before we found out family secrets,

Before careers and children

Before tears and tragedy,

There was innocence and happiness on

Anderson Street.

Look at us—

Three little 'colored girls' in the Sixties

Happily wearing our white all-occasion

dresses

Professionally home-made by Mama's

Cousin Eva—

Mine, a Jackie Kennedy want-to-be suit and

looking older than a pre-teen,

the middle one marked with navy blue

ribbon, and

Kathy grinning while holding Cutie Pie, the

doll, as if her dime-store child was one of

the sisters.

Nine years stretch between the first and last.

The question remains after all these years

past.

Who messed up and turned around?

Heading different directions in life was the

answer found.

Dundee Street Dance Lessons

We danced and we swayed

on Ms. Mattie's sleek kitchen floor.

Black tiles and white tiles reflected our smiles.

Little kids, kin, cousins, and friends

Learning to step

And to turn and to

Hold heads correctly.

Chubby Checker songs were on the radio—

Some tunes fast, some tunes slow.

No harsh words to warp our minds

or twist our tongues.

Twisting hips time was a good old time.

We danced

And we swayed

On a checked kitchen floor-

Took our steps and loved the life that was made.

Taught by the older girls Anice, Claretha, and Harriett Jamison.

Dundee Street Tree

For years, the only part of Dundee

Still standing, still growing was that tree—

Towering tall in memory,

Comforting and shady.

As I pass now, I see small homes

For the homeless and remember me at 13 Dundee.

Reflections from the Diaspora

Hands of Belize
An Eintou in Three Pearls

Hands carve
Hands shape black wood
Hands roast cashews to sell
Hands make fry jack and spread fruit jam
Hands thread, weave, cover heads.
Hands create dolls;
Hands move.

Beat drums.
Hands harvest shells
chiseled into jewelry,
Hands hide lips, cover Creole secrets.
Hands mix up peas and rice,
gather cat-eyes--
stones change.

Hands stir,
mix stew chicken,
polish volcanic rock.
Hands vend to turn stone into bread,
Hail foreigners
Cruising island--
Leaving.

Bus Ride from Caves Branch River

Just when you think
No one could live in that place--
No windows,
No door,
Barely a roof.
Just a few concrete blocks
abandoned and stacked,
boards barely hanging
in case of wind, rain,
or wet seasons of hurricane.
Out front, old tires, a rusty car in parts
Rests on ancient land once cultivated by
Mayan hands…

Just when you think
You, on your puttering tour bus
No one could live in that place,
Four little ones suddenly appear
Running and laughing
In front of their home
as sun sets.

Poetic notes from Teach Abroad experience in
Belize, May 19, 2007

Ashe! Call and Response in B Flat and Bent Notes

The singer, Rachelle Ferrell,

Wears the story

on her long brown peasant skirt

imprinted with images of Africans toiling in

cotton fields,

carrying bundles on heads and shoulders;

brings the story like *Ursa*[6]

Twirls the fabric of America's re-memory .

The singer, Rachelle

Patches blues-filled spirits

On a Sunday at the New York Blue Note –

says, "A connection is made."

"Thank You, Lord"

---

[6] Fictional character in Gayl Jones's novel *Corregidora* about
a blues singer who performs narrations of slavery passed
down from her grandmother.

free-styling and prophesying for

the feminized, the marginalized, the set

aside.

The musician stranger follows the pattern,

reads the drums,

watches the sticks,

listens behind the beat, with the beat,

in the cut.

The actor stranger rooted in Louisiana,

somebody's well-raised son,

Remembers his First Sunday mornings and

is not ashamed.

"Well!" "Preach!"

Tomorrow's sunrise by his side cries,

"Ashe! Ashe!"[7]

"Amen!" Amen!"

The singer, Rachelle

Weaves the word in six and a half octaves.

worries lines,

bends notes for

Diaspora's strangers jazzed together

After a rainy night,

After a heat wave,

After stories of

Love and love undone,

After stories of struggles overcome

Everybody says,

"Ashe! Ashe!"

---

[7] A West African word used to invoke thanks and praise; has the same meaning as *Amen.*

"Yehbo!"

From Isizulu to English

South greets South,

Africa transplanted to Georgia,

"Yehbo" we shout to the rhythm of the rain.

My short, dark brothers from Africa's plain

Teach, then raise my spirit with story, song-

Tap hardened black feet in soft white toe

shoes on a gilded stage.

A beat born out of chiseled rock and social

revolution,

They bring voice to victory—

Sweet, melodic tunes

that reflect on work from sun to moon.

In language of song they teach history of

diamonds mined

That cost freedom lost and time.

Song prophets created from broken

commandments

For profits.

Decades overcome now, twenty-first century

sons

Cry out to this West African, Gullah-rooted

daughter

"Yehbo"

They bring tears to the edge of my soul

Like rain which taps softly on this night.

Place, race, and grace

Meet and greet

"Yehbo"

They overcame to come over seas

To bring tears to the edge of my soul,

Tapping softly like the rain which falls this

night.

"Yehbo"

Written in response to a performance by Ladysmith
Black Mamzambo during the Savannah Music
Festival in May, 2005.

"I Am With You"

Though my dog barks

And your recording machine

stops, skips, and scratches my memory,

"I am with you."

I give you, Ma'am, Ms. Hurston,[8]

The best that I have left of

my voice and verses

on this St. Simon road.

I tell you,

"I don't know, but

I take the message to the slave driver,

---

7 *Photo Credit: Lomax, Alan. "Wallace Quarterman." Library of Congress, Voices from the Days of Slavery Collection, District of Columbia, Accessed 15 May 2013*
https://www.loc.gov/item/2007660094/.
I created this poem by transcribing Mr. Quarterman's words from an interview that was conducted by Zora Neale Hurston when she collected slave narratives in the Gullah Geechee region for the WPA during the Depression. It was a research project in ethnopoetics supervised by Dr. Kenneth W. Sherwood at Indiana University of PA. 20 July 2007

Whoop and holler on the Skidaway Island
plantation:

"The big gun shot!

"The Yankees comin'!"

"Turn the People loose!"

"Now, open the door and let me come in".

I, Wallace Quarterman, born in 1844

was there for the Jubilee,

"in and through the State of Georgia".

Saw them throw down their hoes

And heard the words, "You're free."

"Now, open the door and let me come in."

Come eighty-seven years through all the ups
and downs---
Standing strong on my walking stick
"I say, Baby don't you cry."
Hear me over the scratching and the dog
bark.
Mark my words--
"I am with you
until the world shall end."

River Wit: A Praise Poem for March Haynes

He was March Haynes--

escort to Union soldiers,

Conductor underground,

reader of rivers

where Savannah meets the ocean.

He was March Haynes--

interpreter of tides,

rowing and unloading cargo,

from rice fields to the river

leading liberated lives to Cockspur Island.

He was March Haynes

who possessed wisdom about wildlife

flying, swimming, crawling--

more free—more free than he.

He listened along the marsh

to crickets and bird calls

at Fort Pulaski

with wit as his weapon

and freedom dreams for fuel.

He was March Haynes--

escort to Union soldiers,

Conductor underground,

reader of rivers

where Savannah meets the ocean.

Still Water Realities: Creative Non-Fiction

Dear Carolina:

A Letter of Memories

Dear Carolina,

This letter is a long time coming, but I finally have this moment to pay homage for days out in the country and across the bridge to South Carolina.

Why did I find them so special?

I can see the old homesteads like they were yesterday! Some days we would go to camp meeting at Pilgrim Baptist Church in Bellinger Hill, B'lingy Hill. We were there for the entire day which consisted of several services with Scotts, Wests, Germans, Parkers, and Chalmers families coming from everywhere!

After the singing, the praying, and counting up the money baskets, we would hear the announcement to come eat! Actually, we were all ready before the last "Amen!" The smell of the collard greens, chicken, potato salad, and cakes would start drifting through the air at least a couple hours before.

The men would set up tables and benches right there in the cemetery! I recall the women like my mother Anna Bell, and Aunties Rose, Ruth, and Aire Bell helping with the set up. They would spread those tables with white table cloths and pitchers of ice cold water and lemonade.

In Bellinger Hill, I was exposed at an early age to some of the old traditions that were still practiced in the 1960's and 70's.

As the years evolved, I paid more attention to the stories about the ancestors and the Cummingsville Cemetery. Over 150 years ago after Emancipation, Jane Cummings and Robert Scott and their families acquired several acres of land in what is now Jasper County, South Carolina. As a part of their legacy they deeded a part of this acquisition to the family as a designated cemetery which is still in use today. In recent years, this family legacy has been threatened by outside forces that contribute to the desecration of our historic and holy ground.

The first problem developed several years ago when the descendants were cut-off from access to a part of the path that leads to the South Carolina side of the Savannah River landing where our people were baptized and where religious meetings were held. Without our knowledge, a private home was built on what we thought was public, historic ground. The landowners put up a fence and cut off access to that peaceful spot that African Americans treasure in our history.

Carolina, how could you let that happen?

During summer breaks and on Sundays, we would go further up Highway 17 to visit relatives in Parker's Ferry. I started going about age 5 or 6 so some of the memories might be a little fuzzy. I recall that as soon as we turned off of Highway 17, we were waved in by everyone who spotted us driving in. It was a sign of respect. It was a time when we were all one, big loving Black community. If it were a Sunday visit, we would go from one uncle and aunt to the next. We would turn down long, dusty paths where we would be greeted by warm hugs and kisses.

Every visit was like an educational fieldtrip. I learned how to prime and pump water. I did not care for the sulfur taste which differed from the Savannah city water, but water was water for survival. Even when mixed with one of those flavored drink packets, the taste was still there. We learn and grow from differences.

Before modernization, the outhouse made us city children humble! At most houses, we would walk out back to a wooden mystery building from which we had to chase the chickens first. The little shack was made of wood, also the composition of the seat and the lid over what I guess to this day was just a hole in the ground. Nevertheless, it served its purpose.

First, just getting up in the morning in Parker's Ferry was a simple pleasure. The freshest, coolest breeze flowed through to awaken us along with the rooster's crow. The memory of that fresh, clean air is one I treasure.

Carolina, do you remember how we would spend the day? It was there that I heard some of the most powerful morning prayers. After the wake-up prayers heard throughout Parker's Ferry, the women would be in the kitchen stirring. Sounds of water splashing, pots clinking, and a spoon dropped here and there acted like an alarm clock. Children would just lie there until somebody said something to get us stirring. No matter where we spent the night, we had chores to do. After we got up, we washed the dishes, made the beds, hung up the clothes outside on the line, and swept the hard dirt yard out front. I recall we had to sweep that dirt until it was smooth and trash free! Who does that? Sweep dirt? I learned in later years that it is a West African tradition and another transatlantic survivalism. Of course, we did as we were trained, no mouthing or disrespect. After all the chores, we were on our way to the Crossroads.

The walk was the highlight of our day. For what? To get store-bought things like pickles, hard candy, my favorite chocolate bar, a Butternut, potato chips, Kool-Aid mix, or peaches from the 'Peach Man'. Sometimes kin folks would send for "a dollar's worth of salami," fifty cents worth of bologna, or a loaf of 'light bread.' Along the way, we would stop and pick up cousins—just girls giggling, talking, and wondering about serious life issues that growing up brings on. As we gathered in somebody's living room around the table-top record player, we just knew we were the Supremes. After the dancing and singing, it was time for the walk.

Did anyone ever worry about letting us walk all that way? I mean, it must have been at least 5 miles one way, or it felt that way. Actually, today's GPS, (available technology after our early years, calculates it at 1.83 miles and a 43 minute- walk from houses on Penny Creek Road to the crossroads where the old store used to sit until it was torn down to make room for the expanded highway. Many of us miss that old place. How did we as pre-teens and children cross Highway 17 without one incident? The grown-ups probably started praying as soon as we stepped foot on Penny Creek Road.

After eating and talking our way back, we would drop off the send-by packages. We resumed our adventures in the opposite direction towards Penny Creek Landing. It was just Penny Creek to us, wasn't it? We didn't have any boats. Then, it was a very private gem hidden away in a virtually secluded African-American community— host to our families and the wildlife. As a small child, I did not know about slavery or plantations then. I did not know that the Native Americans were the first to canoe along the Edisto River. We would take a slow, slow, slow walk with warnings ringing through our minds.

"Ya'll look out for snakes!"

We walked until the pavement ran out and we met the cool basin of water that ran perpendicular to the road like the top of a capital T. A thick canopy of trees overhung on both sides. We knew all the rules that the grown-ups had drilled into us.

There must have been a reason for the repetition.

"Look out for snakes!"

"Don't go in dat wata!"

Carolina, you should have seen us inch and inch and inch as close as we could without breaking the "Don go in dat wata" commandment. Not to worry though, our thrill was to skip rocks. After we spent several minutes looking out "to see if anything was moving," we'd begin the contest. Who could get the most skips and make the rock go the closest to the other bank of the river? Sometimes now life is like that rock-skipping contest—trying to get the most out of a situation and make it go a long way.

We would get back safely and ready for the dinner adventure. Carolina, it was there that I recall seeing smoked sausage, beans, and rice cooked on a wood-burning stove. On special occasions on a Sunday, we enjoyed fried chicken. There lies another irony. Chickens chased by us children would sometimes get caught, neck-wringed, plucked, washed, cut-up, seasoned, and deep-fried in hot melted lard seven days later. Carolina, you gave us some of the best okra and butter beans. Whatever the vegetable was, it was spooned over a bed of dry, white rice.

We would end the day as we had begun—helping to clean up. Then it was safe to bed—using the chamber 'pot', sing-songing "The Lord's Prayer" in perfect rhythm, jumping on the bed, and story-telling.

Carolina, those days with you in B'lingy Hill and Parker's Ferry are priceless and precious. My generation relives those days with pride, humor, and even tears. You know about that. Sadly, we have lost so much. We have lost our legal right to visit

Cummingsville Cemetery and stand on the banks of the Savannah River on your side.

We have lost the innocence of Parker's Ferry to the outside world. Penny Creek is overused and littered as a landing by boat owners who say they value the Ace Basin. Gentrification has some homes priced over $200, 000 for just one bedroom. We have fallen victim to addictions, domestic violence, and worse. Too many young are in the graveyard. Don't want to bother you with all that. We need those thundering early morning prayers, Carolina. The outside world came in too hard and too cold. They did not know that Parker's Ferry was, and is, a place for soft, cool breezes.

Mattie's Time

"Oh, no."

"Mama, Mama."

The news came late in the dark after a day's labor.

Before day cleaned Mattie knew she didn't feel well. Should she tell her husband, Abraham? Time continued to pass in the farmhouse in Parker's Ferry, South Carolina. Mattie's pain would not go away. It was the breaking of another day, September 21, 1931. It would begin as usual, but end like no other day expected or ever imagined.

"Y'all boys get on up and don't let me have to tell you again," ordered Abraham their father. He had already said his morning prayers and blessed the house. He had all he needed –his Bible and his whip. They say Reverend Abraham Wilson, Sr. was a tall, black velvet skinned, slender built man who walked and talked with his whip and pistol everywhere he went. He was known everywhere he steered that wagon pulled by his loyal mule, Red, who would nod and automatically stop at homes of members Abraham would pick up for church service or prayer meetings.

This day, he was worried that the cotton in the field would get picked in time. Times were hard during the depression, and the Wilson family was struggling like everyone else in the United States. The state of South Carolina had just passed an act to provide loans to farmers, but what was the chance of colored farmers receiving any of that?

"The world is coming to an end!" Word had come from the city of the signs. There was flooding in China and a deadly earthquake had hit Japan. Colonel Lindberg and his wife had volunteered to fly over to help survey the damage of the quake which killed several poor people. What was important to Abraham Wilson was getting his cotton picked and taken to his cotton gin up Parker's Ferry Road.

It was a fine September fair weather morning south of Charleston. Temperatures were hovering in the high 80's, but there had been some rain. All the sights and sounds were there—the dewy fresh clean air and the rooster crowing. Benjamin, who was Abraham's son and plow hand, reacted to a loud crack.

"What dat?" he asked curiously.

"Somebody shootin' bird…getting' 'e breakfast, Edward, the older plow hand brother answered.

"I wonda what we eatin' this mo'nin'? Benjamin was a hungry teen-aged boy.

The boys got up, washed their faces, and slipped on their shirts, coveralls, and old boots. They obediently walked out back to start the chores. As teenaged boys they were already schooled in feeding animals and milking the cows. The family dog, Boomer, met them at the door.

"Y'all boys be s'hrough by the time I get back. I gon check on yo mama."

Mattie was still in bed, barely able to get herself up.

"Ain'no time to be sick. Dat cotton got to be pick to go to da ma'ket, woman."

"I ain' able, Abraham. My head killin' me. Got a pain on the right side of my head."

"What I say?" Get on up and get 'dere in dat field. And them churn need som'in to eat."

"By now five-year-old Anna Bell was awake tugging on her Mama to get up. She climbed up on the bed to play in her Mama's long hair. This gave Mattie a little strength—along with Abraham's commanding voice.

She was afraid to make him angry, like the night he went to his oldest son William's house and beat him in front of his new wife. He was the master of his own house and that of others up and down Parker's Ferry Road. Mattie pondered all of this as she put wood in the stove to heat a pan of water. She took a cool wash rag and ran it over her light brown skin. Somehow, Abraham even managed for all the children to have his handsome dark complexion, though she did pass on her Edisto Native American-featured nose to Anna, Edward, and Minus, the youngest boy.

She thought of all her 14 living children this morning. She wondered about her 13-year old Nettie, the only other girl besides Anna Bell. Baby Rebecca, James's twin, had not survived. She wondered where her son James was. He had escaped Abraham's wrath some time before—supposedly to the Air Corps.

I wish Nettie was here to help me now, she thought to herself. Nettie had already left home. From Monday to Saturday, many of the Parker's Ferry teens left their own homes to work on a nearby white man's farm-plantation. The extra money gonna help me and Abraham make ends meet, she convinced herself. She wasn't one to say much out loud, for fear that Abraham would not approve.

She went on quickly, nervously to get breakfast ready by the time Abraham and the boys got back in the house. Head throbbing and feeling faint, she struggled to get herself and Anna Bell dressed.

The smell of almost rancid bacon filled the house and drew the boys to the table like flies on a cow's tail. The milk was warm and freshly drawn.

"Lord, thank ya fo the food we 'bout to receive for the nourishment of our bodies. Amen."

After Abraham's grace, the family ate and drank quietly—grits drizzled with grease, bacon from the smoke-house, coffee, and milk. Anna Bell looked at her mama whose complexion was the color of the coffee with the milk and sweet sugar added in. Her daddy was the color of the coffee itself. She picked at her food, but knew she had to eat every drop before her daddy got loud like he did on Sunday mornings when he talked loud in the church.

Mattie washed the dishes, threw the dirty water outside the door, and cleaned up. Time seemed to stand still while Abraham went on out to the cotton field. Mattie's head was throbbing.

"What's wrong, Mama?" You playin' a wobblin' game?"

"No, Anna. Mama just feel dizzy—like the whole world spinnin' 'round and 'round." Go on back in the house and stay with Big Al today." Alice

Youngblood Wilson was married to Abraham's brother Robert, born in 1892. While Robert worked as a logger at the lumber mill, Big Al helped on Abraham's farm. Benjie continued to walk with his mother.

"Mama, you want me to tell daddy?"

"No, Benjie. I be a'right."

They walked quickly—trying to beat the heat of the day. It was still a cool morning, not too hot. Alma, Mattie's oldest grand, was there to help. Mattie, Alma, and Benjie were responsible for a certain section of the cotton field. The head-wrapped women were ready. Benjie carried the cotton sack.

All Mattie could think about was working to Abraham's satisfaction—getting the cotton picked on time, making supper on time…

Time…

She had no more. The pain. The sun. The cotton field. With Alma and Benjamin by her side, her time stopped.

She dropped.

Benjamin could not catch her. Alma could not scream loud enough. The word spread throughout

Parker's Ferry like a communion plate passed from soul to soul.

"Rev. Wilson wife drop dead in 'de field. One 'o 'e sons been right 'dere."

"Yeah, mon, I hear."

"E son Edward and another man don gon to tell Nettie."

"How Rev. Wilson do'in?"

"Mon, 'dey tell me 'e make dat woman go out dere in dat field sick."

"For true?"

"Say she beg 'im for help."

The next day, the Trailways bus stopped at Parker's Ferry Road where it intersects with what is now Highway 17. A young man on board departed wearing an Air Corps uniform. He watched a crowd of people gathered along the road. Later, James discovered it was the funeral of his mother. He was coming to see her, but time did not wait. He missed her and her funeral due to a misbeat of time. They buried Mattie—40-years old, mother of 14 living.

The cotton kept on growing. Abraham went on working and preaching--appearing tall, strong, and tough.

Time continued to pass and the rest of the family would live and work and feel Mattie's pain.

New Days—Day Clean

Apology: A Strand of Seven Eintou Pearls

Wounded
Betrayed and sold
For 'God', dollars, power.
Centuries past. force life present
Acknowledged formally.
Heritage hurt--
Resolved?

Forgive
Whips, bits, strippings--
"atrocities", they say.
Turn 'round, face ghosts, confess to heal.
Descendants: dialogue
ink on paper.
Fair deal?

Erase
Mem'ry of fight?
Flight down trails and underground rails?
No! Recall, reclaim, redefine.
We left behind decide.
Keep legacies--
Declare.

Narrate
and reparate
resources; seek the south's
Jim Crow children—separated.
Amendments? Not enough.
Apology?
Pay now!

Dancing in the Dust

We hear their music and don't listen;

Don't realize the song of the griot has

Turned capitalistic and out of rhythm.

Now we see our children twisting their bodies

in confusion.

Not knowing love, they settle for limitations,

Perform imitations of video violence and

Display acts of delusion

as corporate hands spin and pull strings.

We sit and wait and watch our children

With sadness, too much in shock to cry as they

grind out values passed from shore to ship to shore

Stepping on a heritage which offers decency.

We, Africans in America, descend from a place

where dance is done for ceremony and celebration.

While we fight to teach our new generations,

Some of them are leaving us

Dancing in the dust…

Fifth Generation Son, Dedan
A Tritina for Vision

You are the next in line, the fifth
one delivered from a proud warrior
generation,
Gushed forth from an African seeded
daughter and son.

You are the dream come true, grand son
Descending from men whose defense was
the fifth,
From Laboring women singing and praying
for your generation.

Receive now this endangered generation.
Blanket and Liberate our artist and worker
son.
It is time to feed and plead *for* the fifth.

Walk reconciled and take big steps, my
grand fifth generation son.

*Dedicated to my grandson Dedan Kimathi and his
father Dedan Kinyatti, both named after strong
men.*

Come, Day Clean*

A Ntata- A Poetic Outcry

Come, day clean!
Over southern trees evergreen,
Rise up over us with new hopes;
Leave worry in last night's dark and low.
Spread light over us lowly like a balm.
With laughter and lore, help our spirits calm.

With just a touch of dew,
let this be the day our dreams come for true!
Come, day clean!

Satisfy this hunger with fat and lean,
Light these roads of life to help us cope
With injustice just drylongso.
Fight our suffering under the southern palm
With a shout, with an "Oh, Lordy", with a
psalm!

With just a touch of dew,
let this be the day our dreams come for true!
Come, day clean!

*Day clean is an expression from Gullah culture
which refers to dawn or sunrise. It is still used to
this day.*

Made in the USA
Columbia, SC
10 June 2020